Nature Walk

Seeds

by Rebecca Stromstad Glaser

Bullfrog Books

Ideas for Parents and Teachers

Bullfrog Books let children practice reading informational texts at the earliest reading levels. Repetition, familiar words, and photo labels support early readers.

Before Reading
- Discuss the cover photo. What does it tell them?
- Look at the picture glossary together. Read and discuss the words.

Read the Book
- "Walk" through the book and look at the photos. Let the child ask questions. Point out the photo labels.
- Read the book to the child, or have him or her read independently.

After Reading
- Prompt the child to think more. Ask: What seeds have you seen? How do seeds grow?

Bullfrog Books are published by Jump!
5357 Penn Avenue South
Minneapolis, MN 55419
www.jumplibrary.com

Library of Congress Cataloging-in-Publication Data
Glaser, Rebecca Stromstad.
Seeds / by Rebecca Stromstad Glaser.
p. cm. -- (Bullfrog books: nature walk)
Summary: "Describing several examples of seeds, this photo-illustrated nature walk guide shows very young readers how to identify seeds and tells how the seeds spread. Includes photo glossary"--Provided by publisher.
Includes bibliographical references and index.
ISBN 978-1-62031-029-8 (hardcover : alk. paper)
Seeds--Juvenile literature. I. Title.
QK661.G57 2013
575.6'8--dc23   2012009110

Series Designer   Ellen Huber
Book Designer   Ellen Huber
Photo Researcher   Heather Dreisbach

Photo Credits: All photos by Shutterstock except: Alamy, 9, 23tl; Dreamstime, 17, 20t; Getty Images, 10, 20b; iStockphoto, 5, 8b, 15, 16t, 19, 23br; Veer, 1

Printed in the United States of America at Corporate Graphics in North Mankato, Minnesota.
7-2012/PO 1123

10 9 8 7 6 5 4 3 2 1

Table of Contents

Looking for Seeds

Let's go on a
nature walk.

Do you see
any seeds?

5

An acorn drops. Plop!

It will grow
an oak tree.

A maple
seed spins.

It will grow
a maple tree.

burr

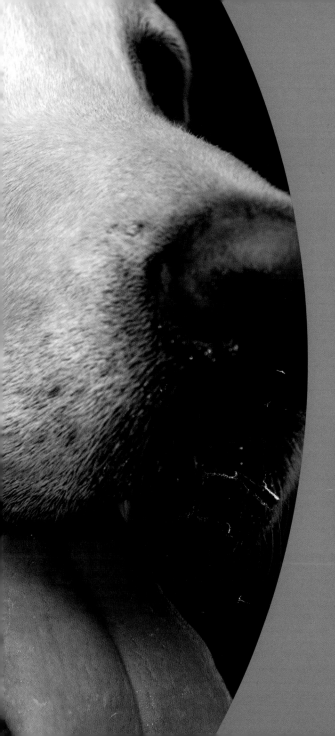

A burr sticks
to fur.

It will grow
a flower.

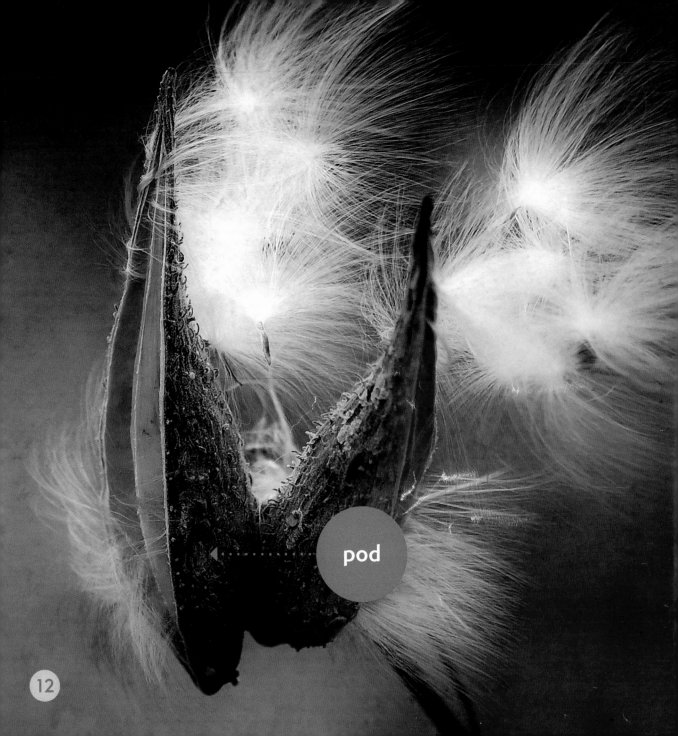

pod

A milkweed pod splits.
Seeds blow away.

They will grow
milkweed plants.

A dandelion
seed blows
in the wind.

It will grow a dandelion.

15

A lotus grows in water.
Its seeds float away.

They will grow a flower.

A pinecone opens.
Seeds are inside.

They will grow
a pine tree.

Not all the seeds will grow.
An animal may eat them first!

20

Watch a Seed Grow

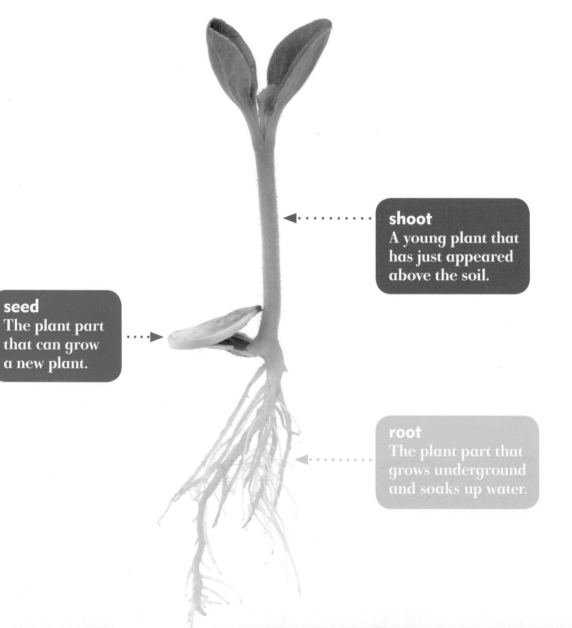

shoot
A young plant that has just appeared above the soil.

seed
The plant part that can grow a new plant.

root
The plant part that grows underground and soaks up water.

Picture Glossary

acorn
The seed of
an oak tree.

pinecone
A part of a
pine tree that
holds seeds.

burr
The seed of a
thistle, which has
small hooks that
catch on things.

pod
A part of a plant
that holds seeds
and opens to
release them.

Index

To Learn More

Learning more is as easy as 1, 2, 3.

1) Go to www.factsurfer.com

2) Enter "seeds" into the search box.

3) Click the "Surf" button to see a list of websites.

With factsurfer.com, finding more information is just a click away.